GRANDPA Kevin's

really kinda strange,
somewhat bizarre,
and overly unrealistic...

BOOK

of

COLOR

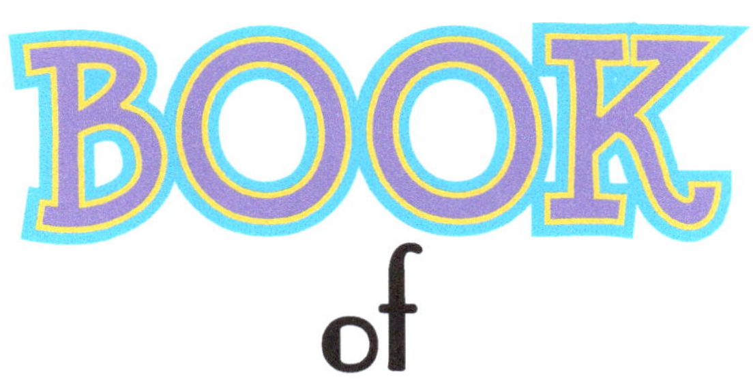

by
Kevin J. Brougher
& Lisa M. Santa Cruz

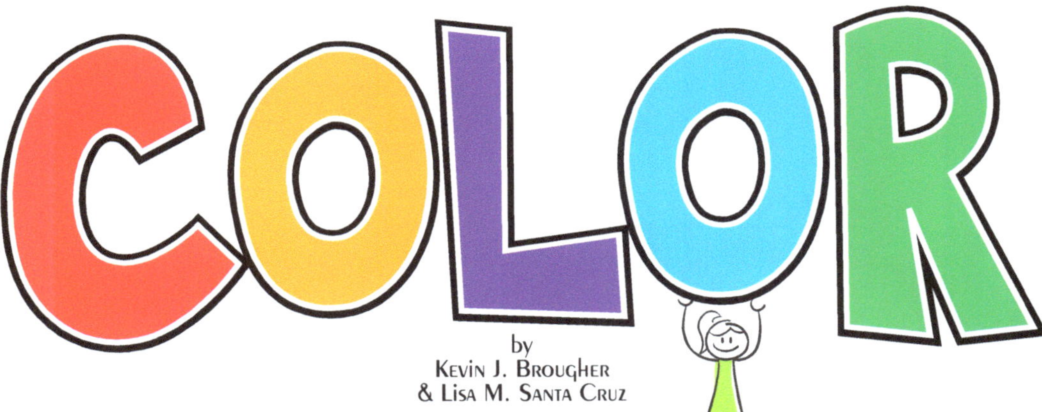

Missing Piece Press, LLC

Grandpa Kevin's...Book of Color

Other Publications from Missing Piece Press

BOOKS

Thinklers! 1 : *A Collection of Brain Ticklers!*
Thinklers! 2 : *More Brain Ticklers!*
Thinklers! 3 : *Even More Brain Ticklers!*
Thinklers! 4 : *Full-Color Brain Ticklers!*
History Mysteries : *A New Twist on Time-Lines*
State Debate : *50 Unique Playing Cards and 50 Games*
Number Wonders : *A Collection of Amazing Number Facts!*
Dreams, Screams, & JellyBeans! : *Poems for All Ages*
The Storybook : *A novel for ages 10 on up*
Science Stumpers : *Brain-Busting Scenarios...Solved with Science*
Algebra Summary Sheets : *Posters to Promote Proficiency*
Reindolphins : *A Christmas Tale*
Who Says Hoo? : *A Book for Babies & Toddlers*
Grandpa Kevin's ABC Book : *Really Kinda Strange...ABC Book*
Number Fun! : *A Book of Counting and Numbers for Toddlers*
Who's Waiting for You? : *A Book of Animal Clues for Toddlers*
The Arizona Book : *An Arizona Introduction*

...and MORE!

GAMES

Frazzle : *A Frenzied Game of Words*
ShanJari : *An African Game of Sequence and Strategy*
Whew! : *Words, Wits, Whims & Woes!*
TooT! : *A Nerdy Little Game*
Blam! : *A Different Card Game*
DICE Blam! : *A Different Dice Game*
Word Nerd : *A Quick-Witted Word Game*
Bunco BUDDIES! : *The BETTER Bunco Game*
Take Twelve : *The Token Taking Game*
CRUMMY : *The Criss-Cross Rummy Game*
Round About : *A Little Thinking - A LOT of FUN!*
Whole Enchilada : *It All Adds up to FUN!*
Besto : *An Animal Matching Game*
Fifty Nifty : *United States Playing Cards & Games*
The Get-to-Know-You Game : *Fun for Families & Friends*
GRID : *The Tic Tac Toe * Tac Toe * Tac Toe Game*

...and MORE!

A Little Thinking
...a LOT of FUN!

Missing Piece Press, LLC

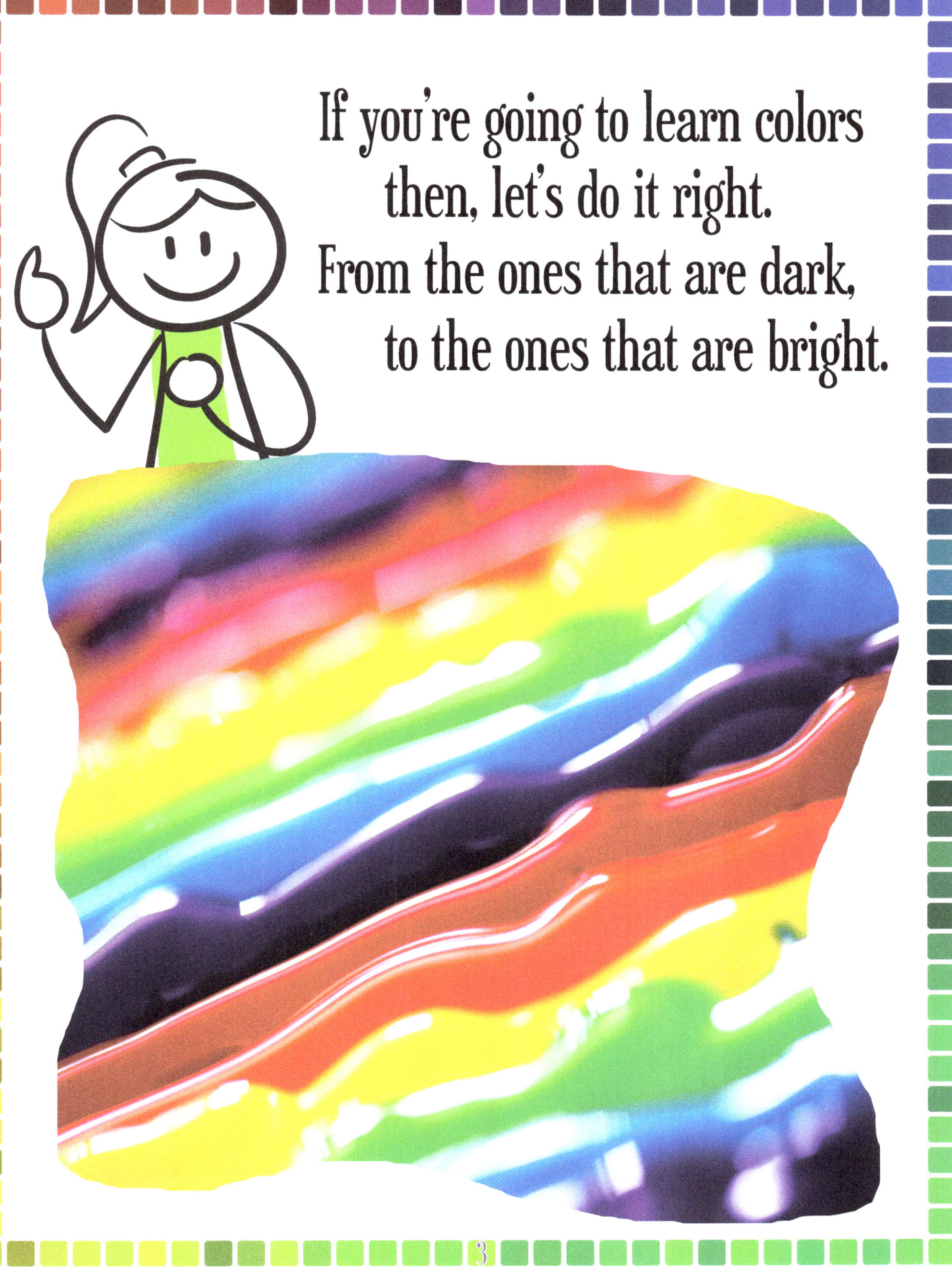

If you're going to learn colors
then, let's do it right.
From the ones that are dark,
to the ones that are bright.

We'll start with the basics.
Though, you might not suspect,
that the subject of color
could be so complex!

But, the first part is easy -
three colors to know.
RED, BLUE and YELLOW.
See them below?

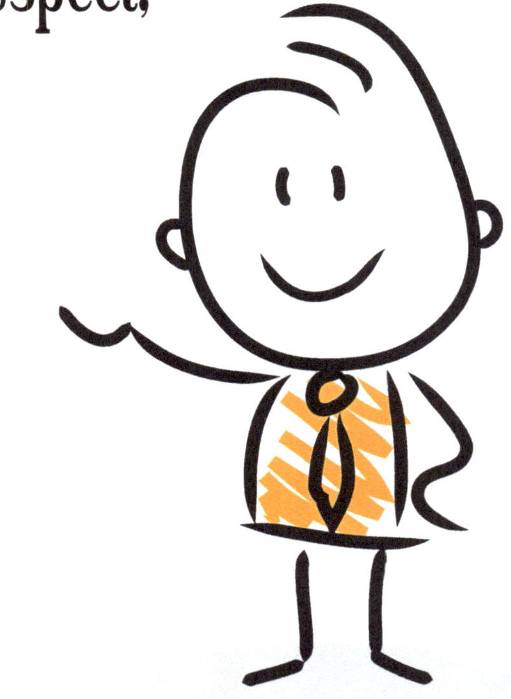

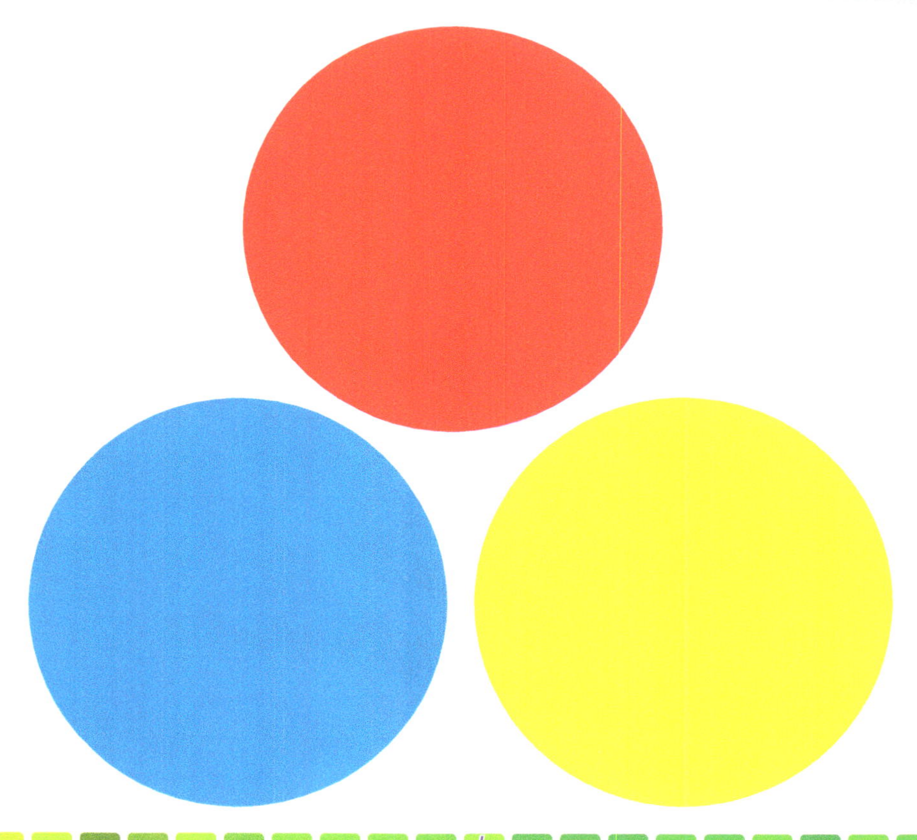

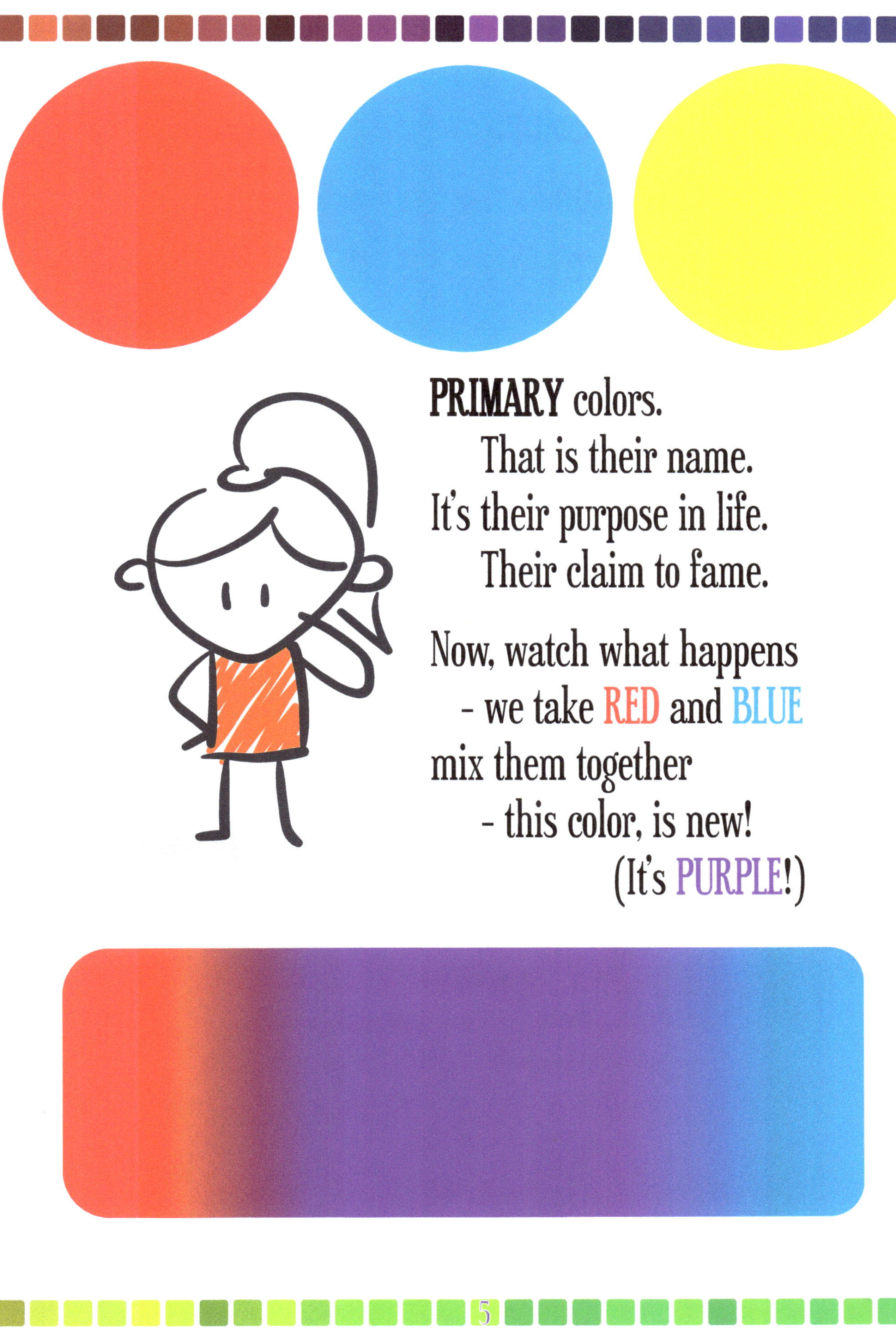

PRIMARY colors.
That is their name.
It's their purpose in life.
Their claim to fame.

Now, watch what happens
- we take RED and BLUE
mix them together
- this color, is new!
(It's PURPLE!)

It's a **SECONDARY** color!
GREEN is one, too.
GREEN is a mixture
    of YELLOW and BLUE.

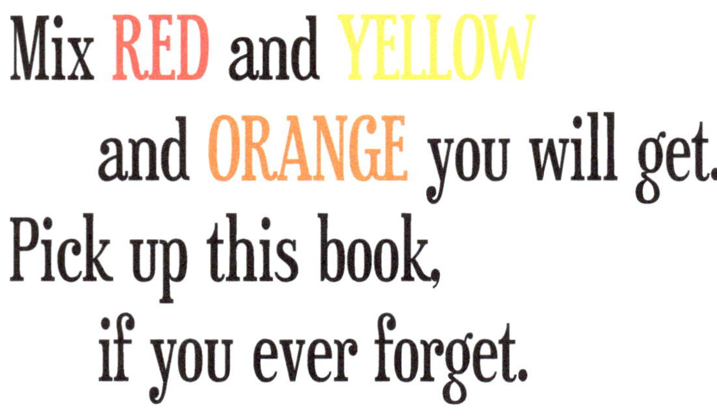

Mix RED and YELLOW
    and ORANGE you will get.
Pick up this book,
    if you ever forget.

If you mix them all,
    you don't hold back –
you're going to see,
    it all turns to black!

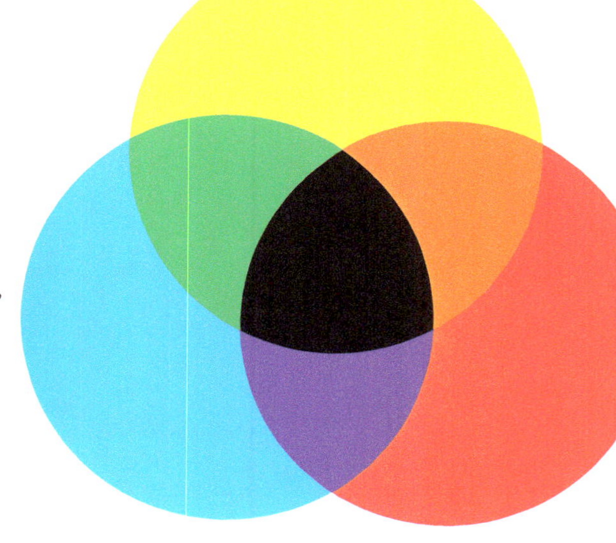

Primary Colors :

Cannot be made from mixing other colors.

RED	YELLOW	BLUE

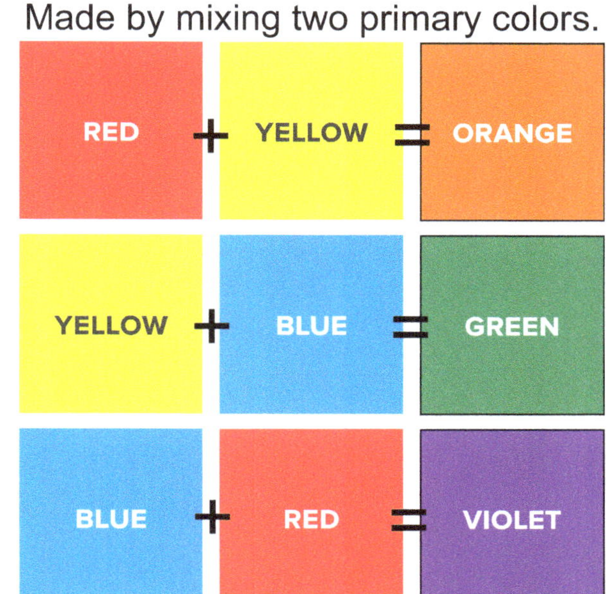

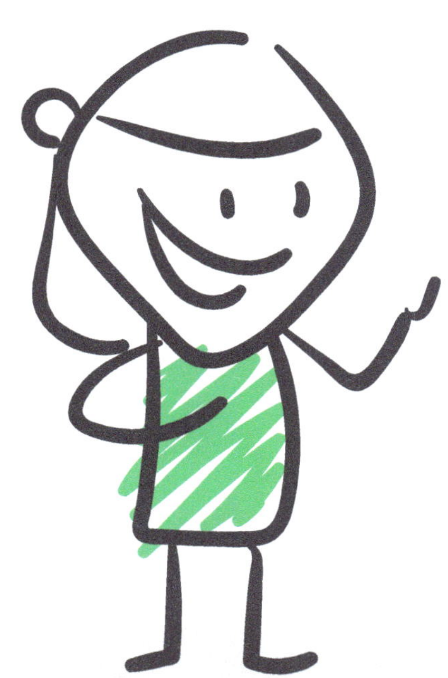

But, these are the **PRIMARIES**
when **PAINT** is the source.
It's a little bit different
when **LIGHT** is the force.

Now, it's not much different.
It's RED, GREEN and BLUE.
There's a few other things
that are surprising and new.

When you overlap GREEN
     with a beam of bright RED,
you would think you'd get BROWN -
     you get YELLOW instead!

If you take all three colors
     in beams of bright light -
mix them together -
     behold, you get WHITE!

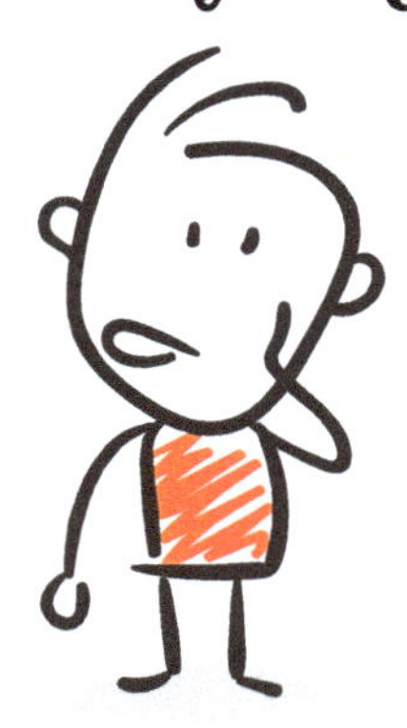

T.V. screens
     use RGB   (RED - GREEN - BLUE)
ALL of the colors
     made from these three.

But, **IF** you are using
        a printing machine
to print a book
        or a magazine -
they use **FOUR** colors
        C M Y K
They can make ALL colors
        and shades of GRAY.

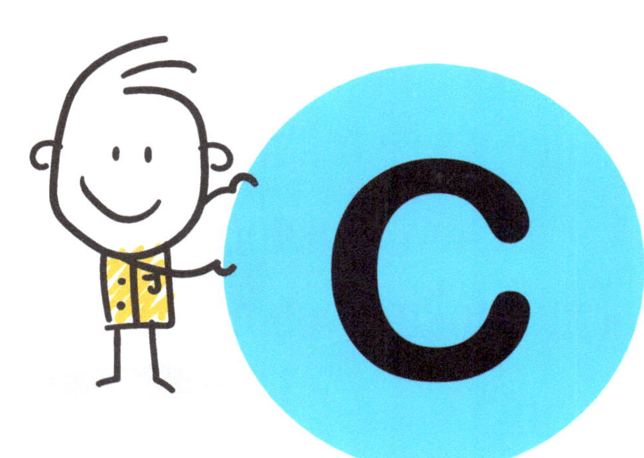
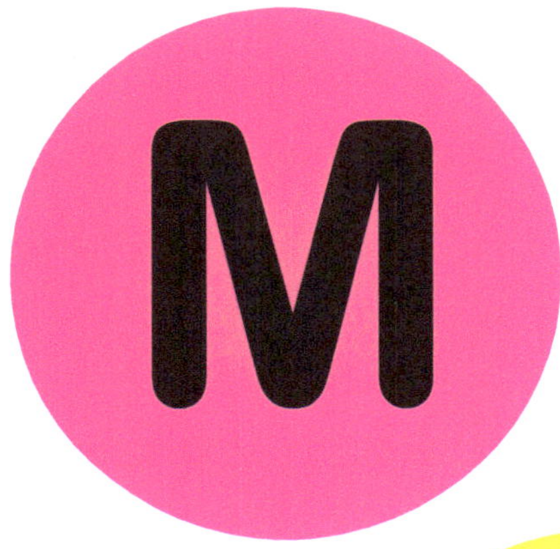

C is for **CYAN** -
        a bright type of blue.
M is for **MAGENTA** -
        A light-red, though and through.
Y is for **YELLOW**
        But, what's out of whack -
K is the letter
        the use for **BLACK!**

Since we're talking 'bout COLOR,
   I know of some words,
I'm thinking you might
   never have heard.

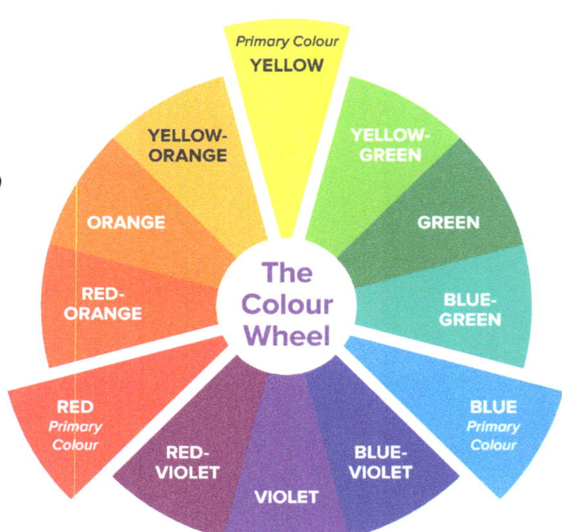

The first one is HUE.
   You can use it instead
of the word - COLOR.
   Like, that HUE is RED.

There's also VALUE.
   But, what might be unknown,
VALUE includes :
   SHADE, TINT & TONE.

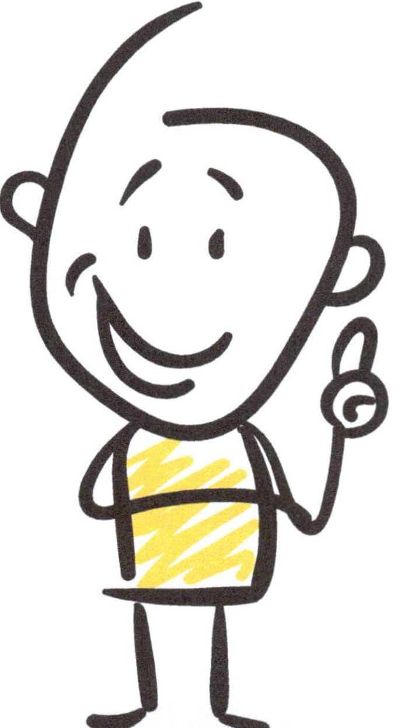

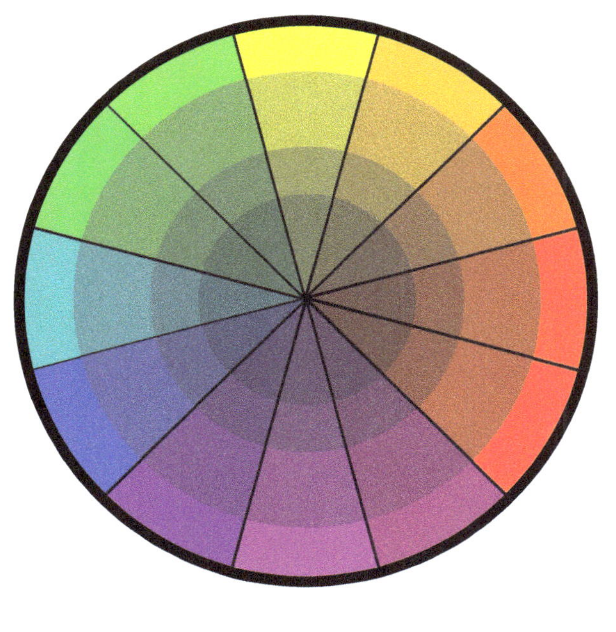

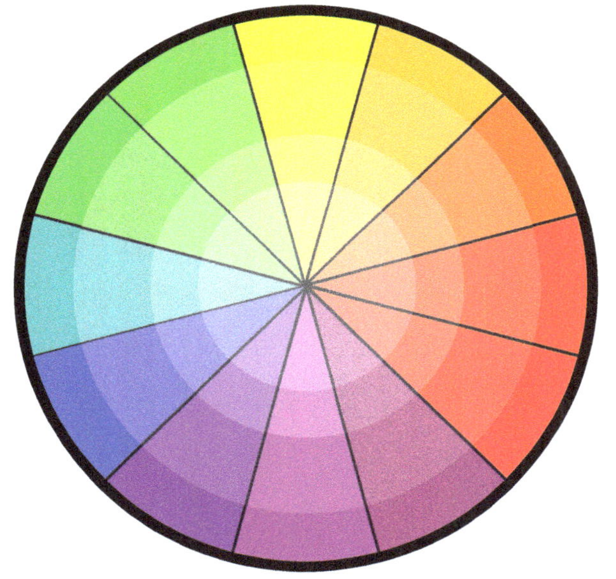

SHADE is a HUE
    that's changed just a bit.
You add some BLACK
    and you have to admit...
that the HUE is darker.
    It's subtle but, clear.
Less intense -
    is how it appears.

But, what about TINT ?
    You guessed it - add WHITE!
All colors become
    a little more bright.

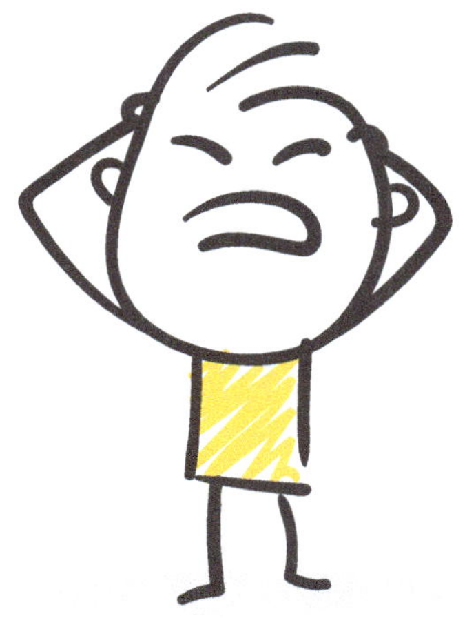

TONE can be tricky.
    It's sole claim to fame -
is it has so many -
    so many names!

TONE's also called BRILLIANCE,
    or CHROMA, it's true,
SATURATION, one more,
    INTENSITY, too.
They ALL mean the same,
    whichever you say,
all describe
    the amount of GRAY.

So, SHADE, TINT & TONE
    describe LIGHT and DARK
Look below...
    is my last remark.

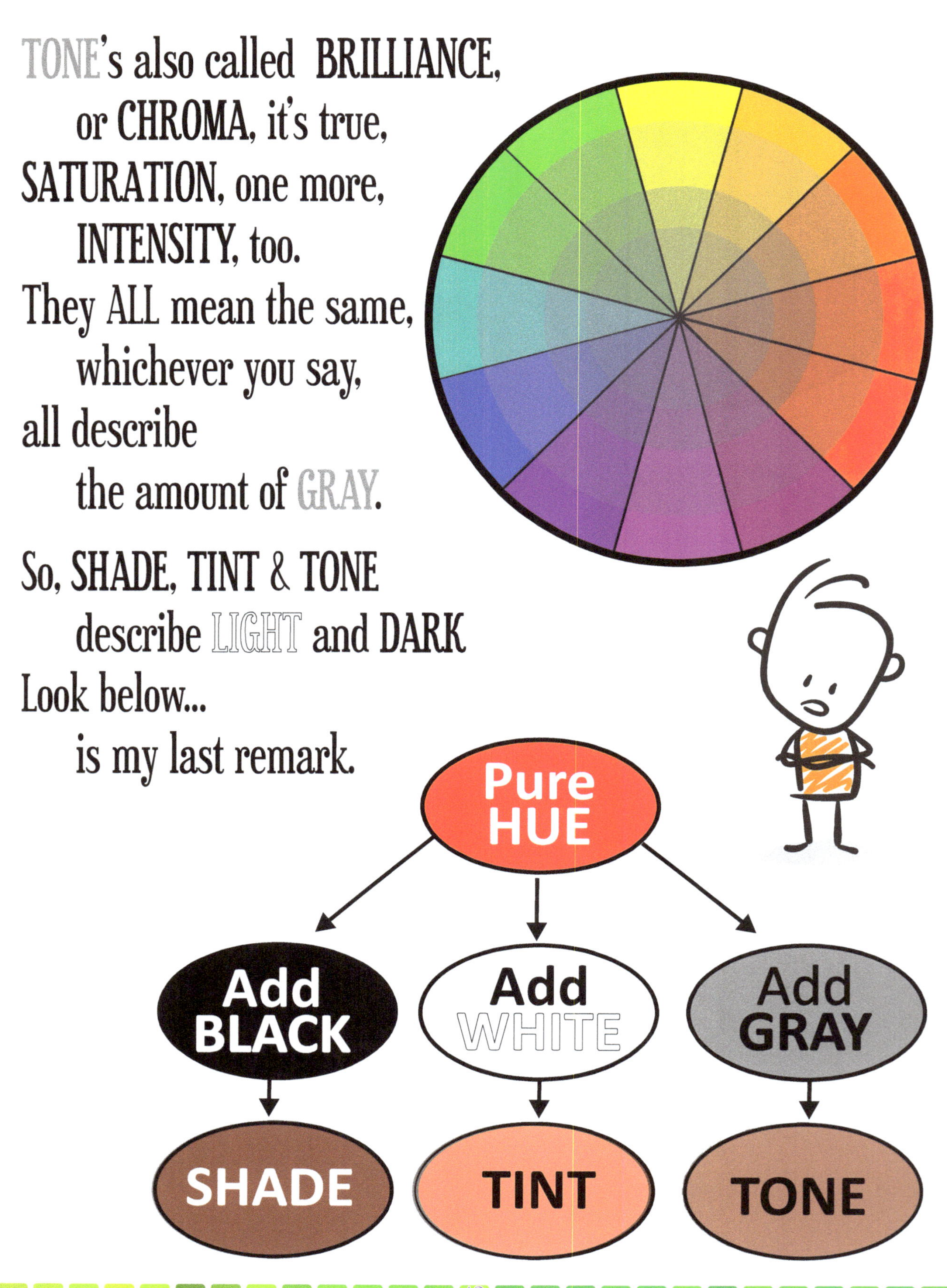

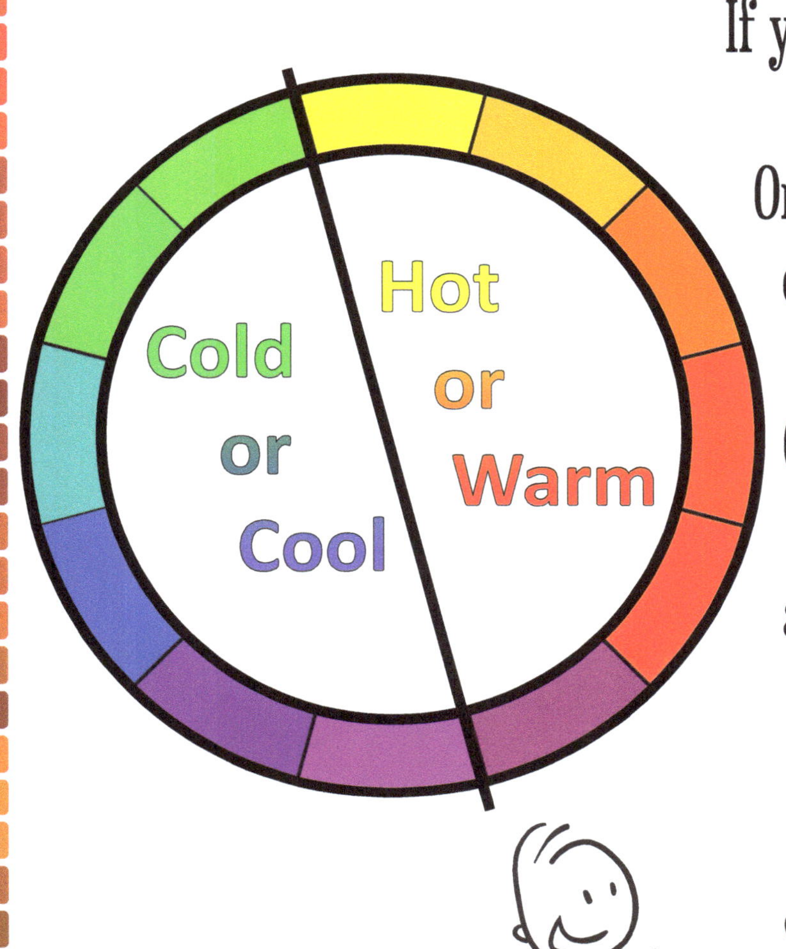

If you look at this wheel
    there's more here to learn.
One side has colors
    of flames that burn.

On the other half side,
    oh, yes, sure enough -
are colors of plants
    and other cold stuff.

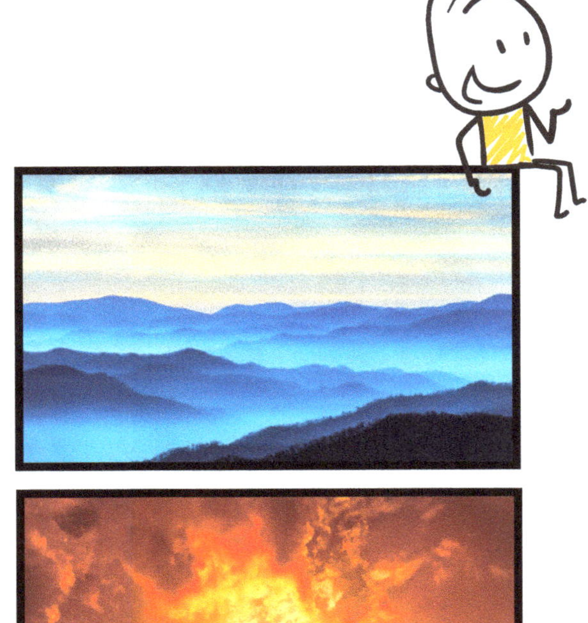

So, HOT or COLD -
    WARM or COOL
are other words
    we use as a tool
to help describe colors
    and what they can do.
How they help set a tone.
    Or, create a new mood!

We need to discuss
color **SCHEMES** now.
The what and the why
and, maybe, the how.

They're kind of big words -
COMPLIMENTARY is first.
It's a bit like if
a color's reversed!

So, start with a color
then, the opposite side -
is what's **COMPLIMENTARY**.
But, what's side-by-side?

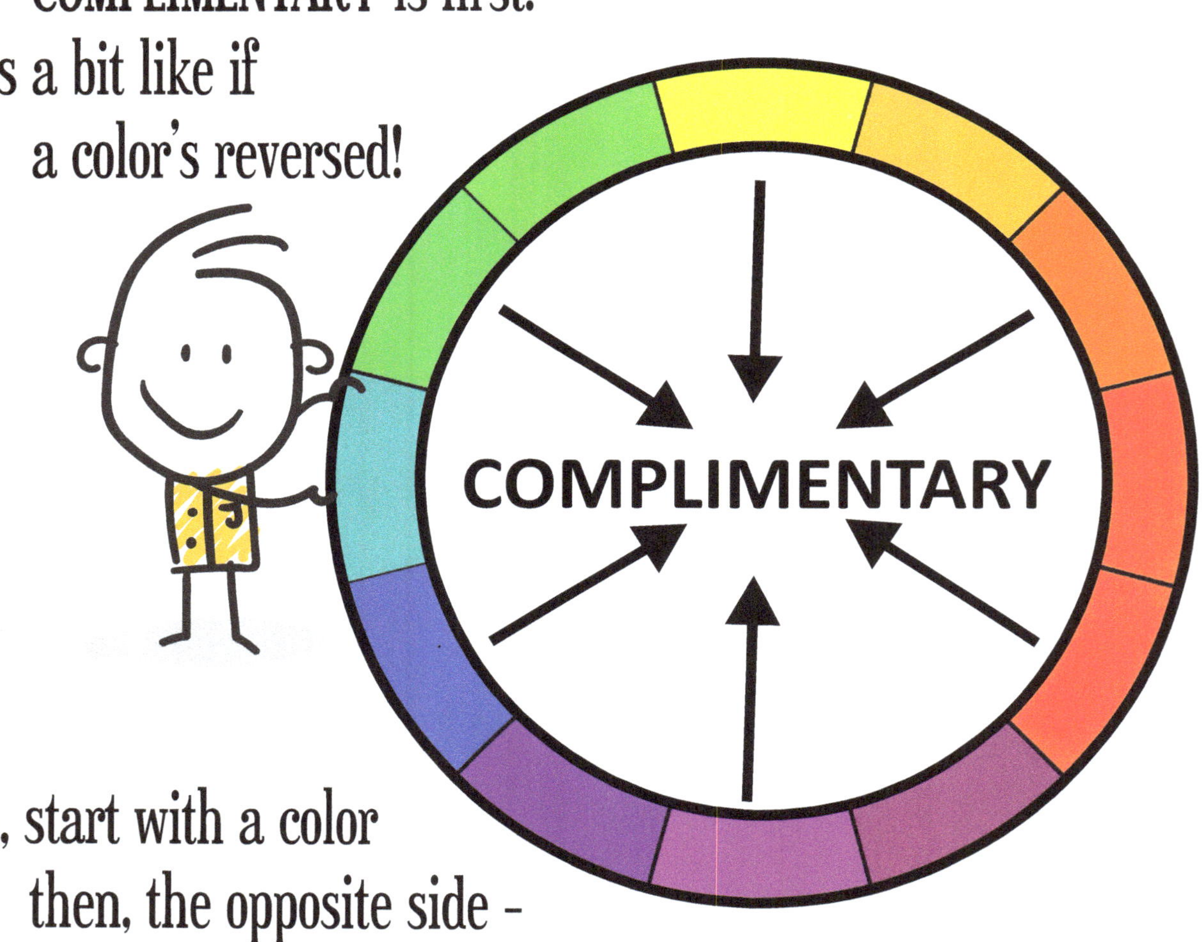

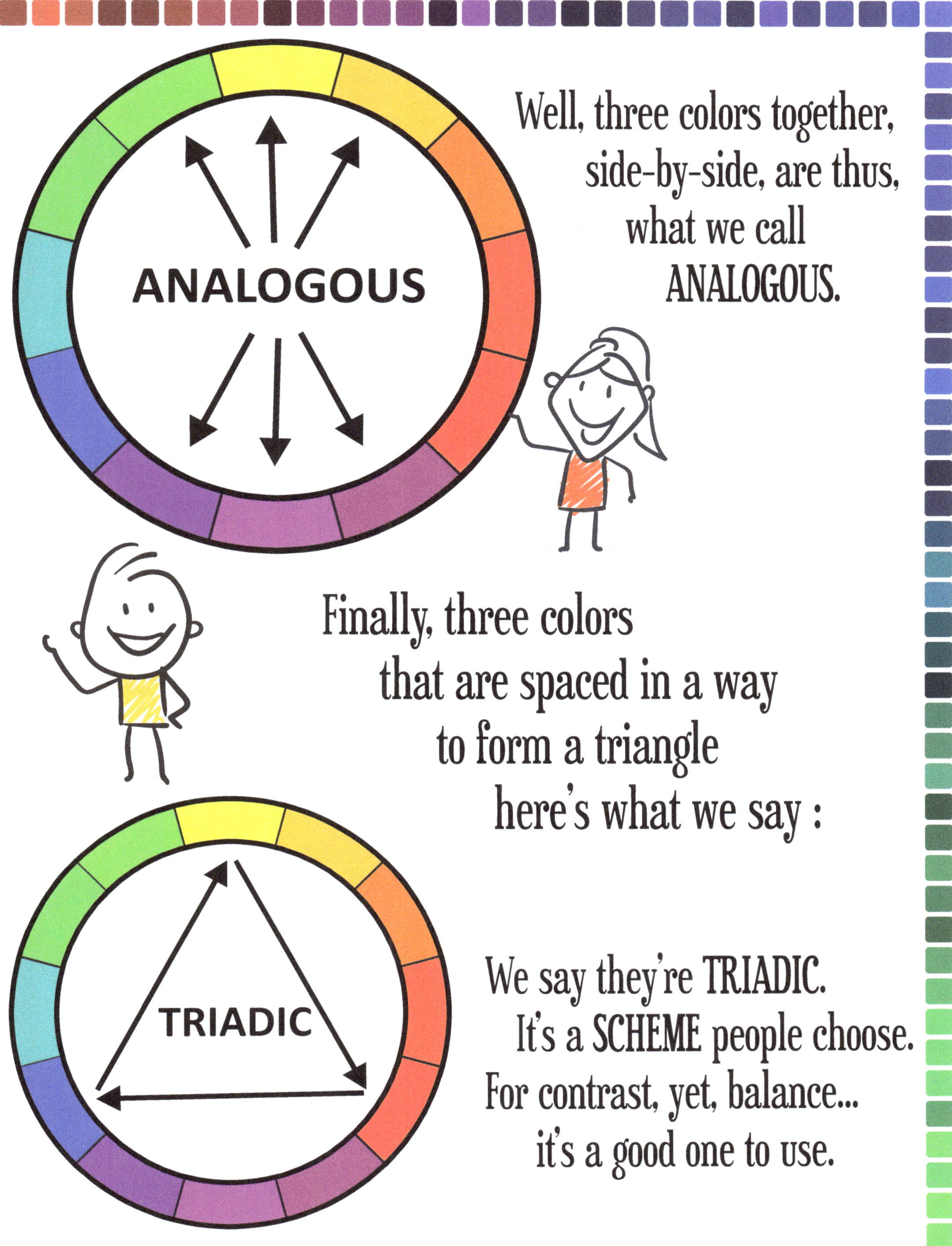

Well, three colors together,
side-by-side, are thus,
what we call
ANALOGOUS.

Finally, three colors
that are spaced in a way
to form a triangle
here's what we say :

We say they're TRIADIC.
It's a SCHEME people choose.
For contrast, yet, balance...
it's a good one to use.

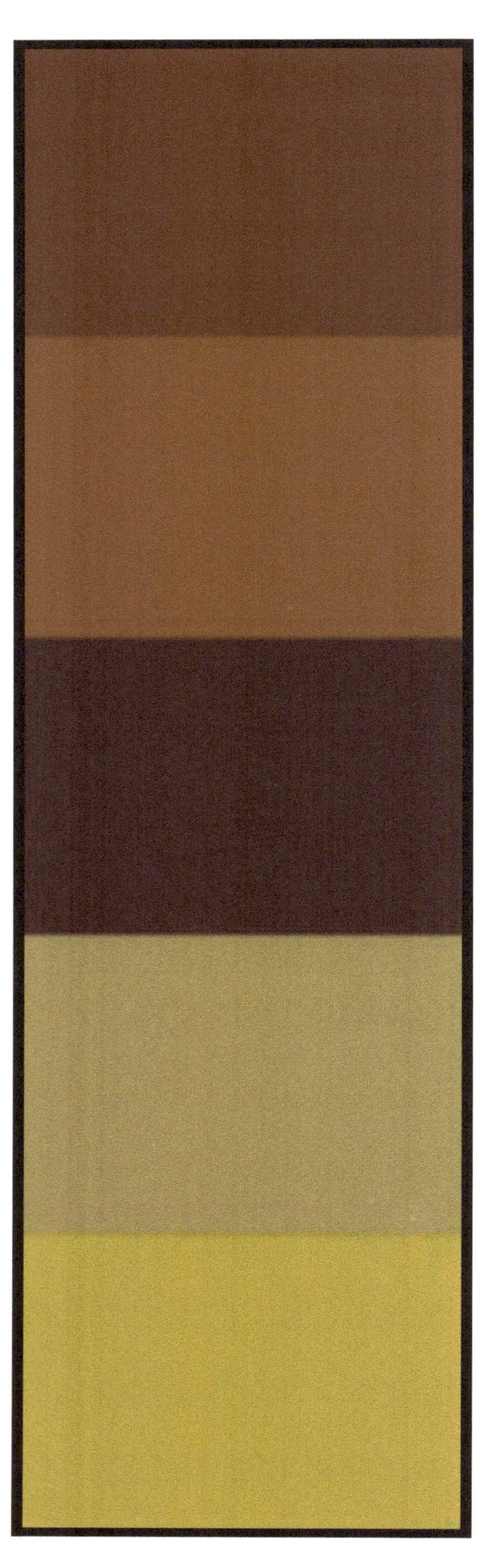

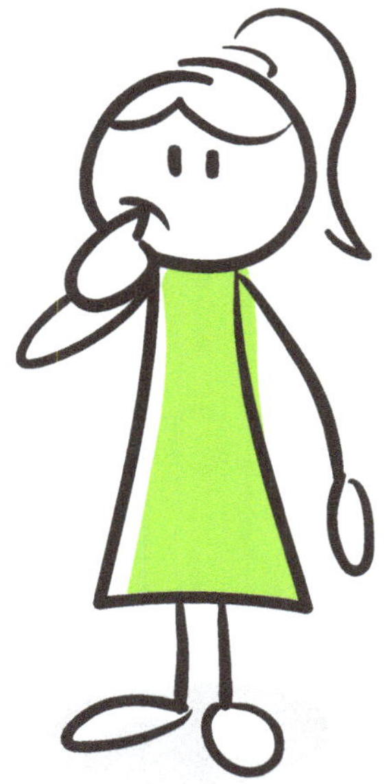

There are some colors
  NOT found on the wheel.
They're NATURAL colors
  and, here is the deal :

They're browns and tans
  and creams and grays.
NEUTRAL colors
  is another phrase.

The colors we see
we see with our eyes -
from the green in the grass
to the blue in the skies.

There's wavelengths beyond,
beyond our gaze.
Like GAMMA, X
and U.V. rays.

It's a very narrow,
narrow band
that our eyes take in
and understand.

But our eyes can't see
ALL of the light.
The **SPECTRUM** we see
is narrow and tight.

We can't see INFRARED
or MICROWAVE light.
And RADIO WAVES
aren't visibly bright.

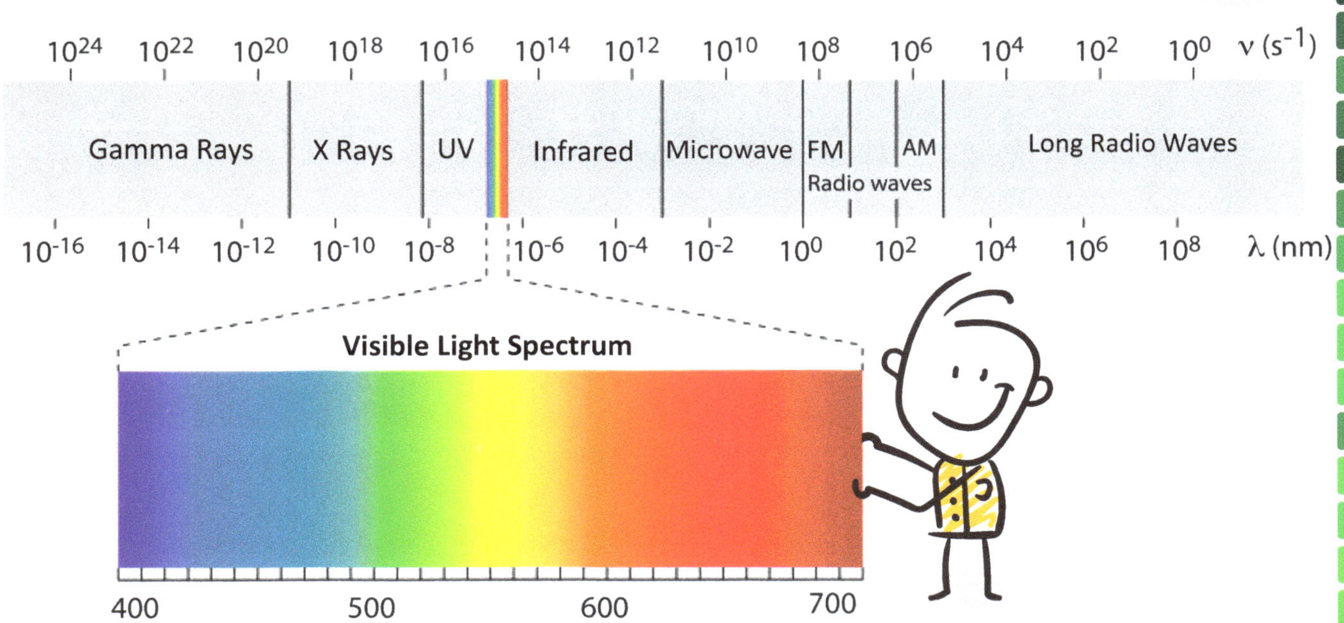

Let's move on
    to something that's fun!
The names of RED.
    There's more than one!

Take a look.
    Learn something new.
When you are done,
    we'll move on to BLUE.

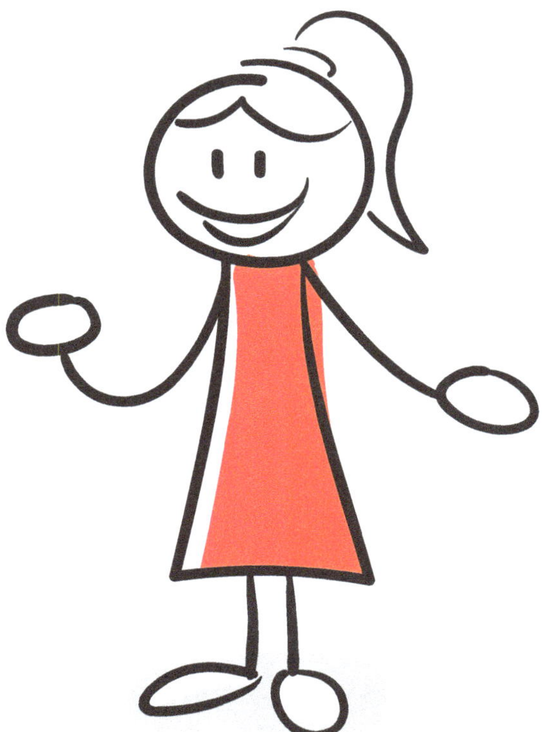

REDS

| Barn Red |
| Burgundy |
| Candy Apple |
| Carmine |
| Chili |

Desire

Ferrari

Fire Brick

Hibiscus

Imperial Red

Indian Red

Mahogany

Maroon

Persian

Raspberry

Redwood

Rust

Salmon

| Sangria |
| Scarlet |
| U.S. Flag |
| Vermillion |

Look at these names
for all kinds of BLUES.
Which is your favorite?
You get to choose!

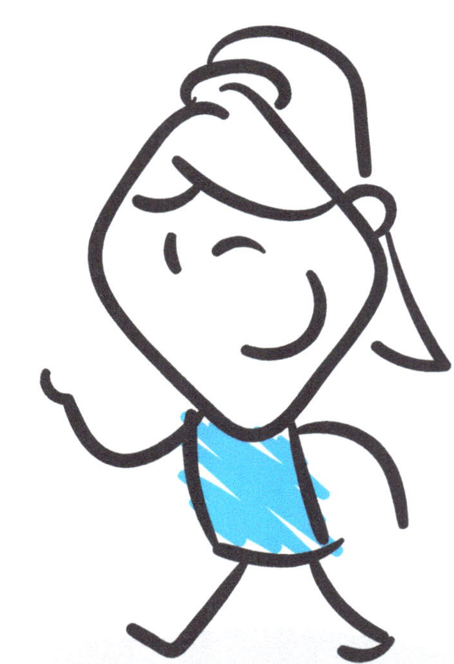

BLUES

| Air Force Blue |
| Alice Blue |
| Azure |

Baby Blue

Carolina

Celeste

Cobalt

Cornflower

Cyan

Denim

Duke

Egyptian

Electric

Indigo

Iris

Navy

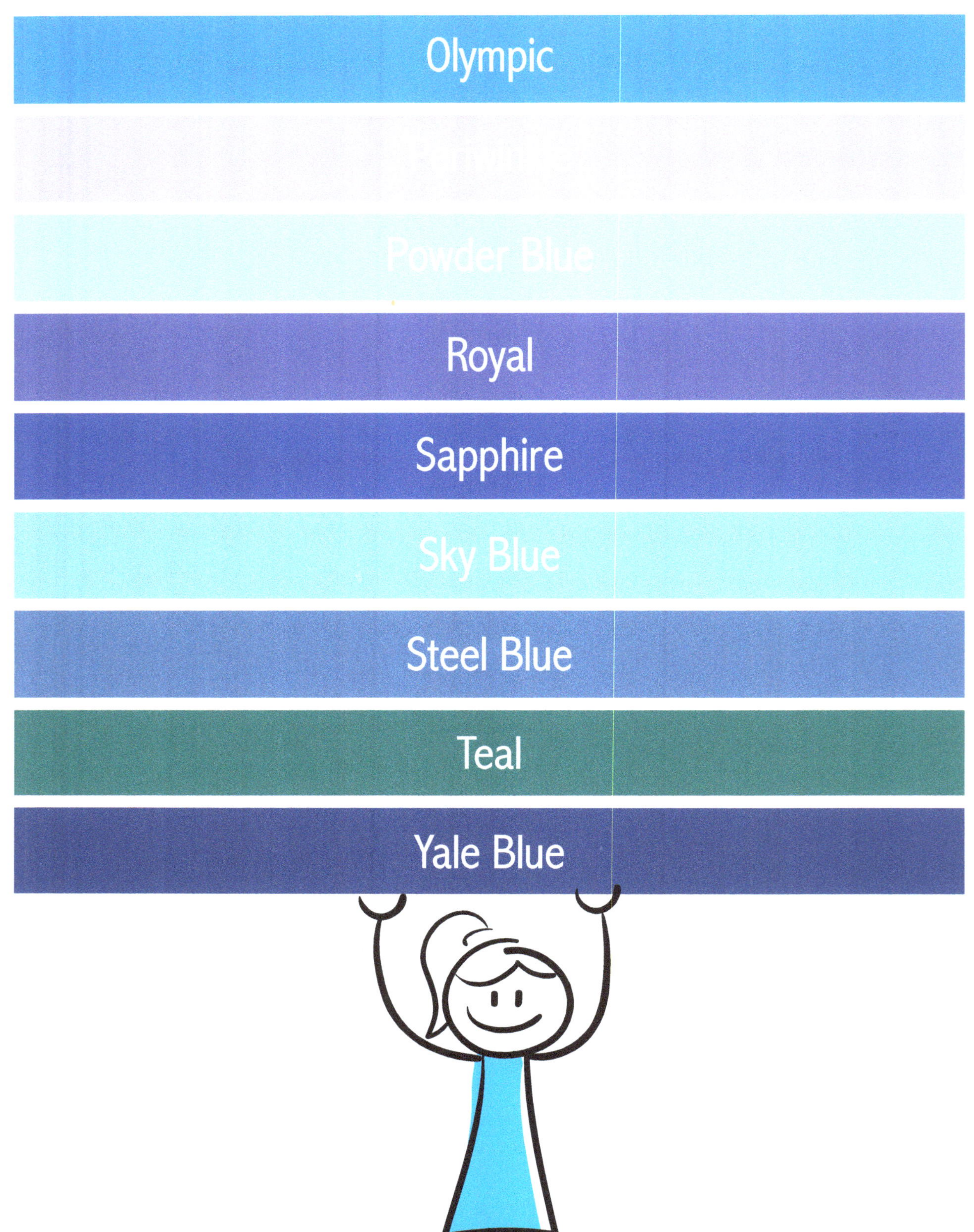

Olympic
Powder Blue
Royal
Sapphire
Sky Blue
Steel Blue
Teal
Yale Blue

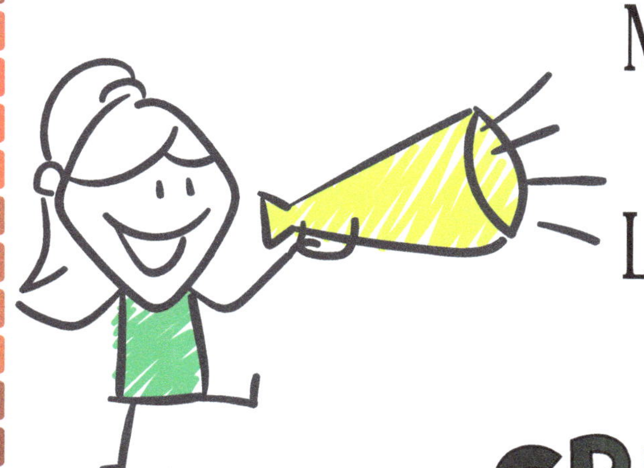

GREENS

Army
Asparagus
Camouflage Green
Chartreuse
Electric Green
Emerald
Fern
Forest
Hunter

Jade

Kelly

Lime

Moss

Mint

Myrtle

Olive

Pine

Sacramento

Sage

Sea green

Shamrock

Tea green

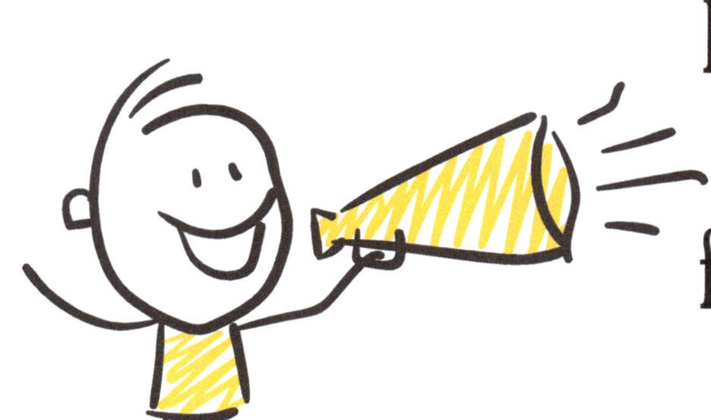

YELLOWS

Amber

Apricot

Banana

Bumblebee

Cream

Corn

Ecru

Egg Nog

Flax

Goldenrod

Laguna

Lemon

Maize

Mellow

Mustard

Peach

Pineapple

Saffron

Straw

Troombone

Tuscany

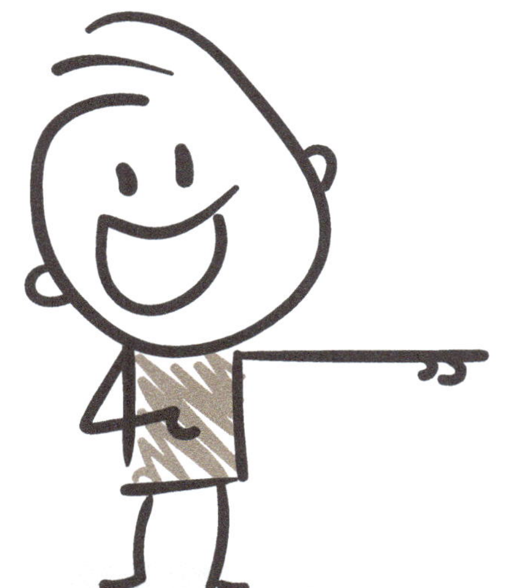

Finally some names,
some names of BROWN.
From the bark for trees -
to the dirt in the ground.

BROWNS

Auburn

Beige

Brunette

Carmel

Cedar

Chocolate

Cinnamon

Coffee

Copper

Espresso

Gingerbread

Hickory

Khaki

Mocha

Peanut

Pecan

Russet

Sepia

Syrup

Tan

Walnut

Now we'll explore,
    and you'll get to read
The phrases with color.
    You will - indeed!

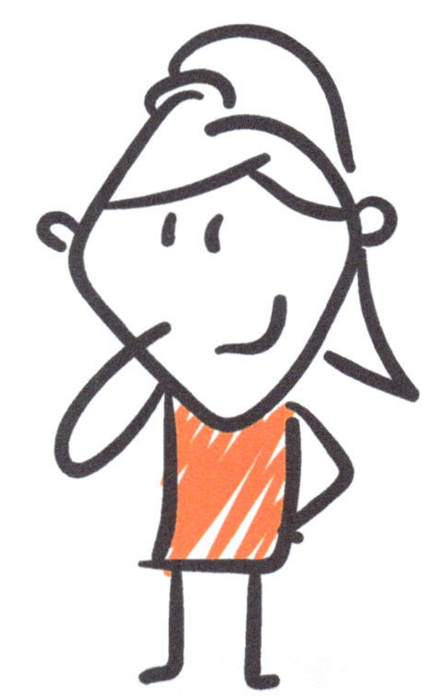

They're used in language
    in so many ways.
They're used in songs,
    stories and plays!

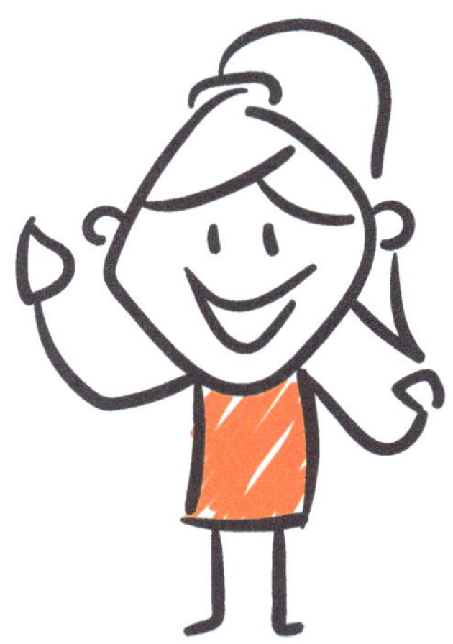

We'll start with RED.
    Look and explore.
These are just some.
    There are so many more!

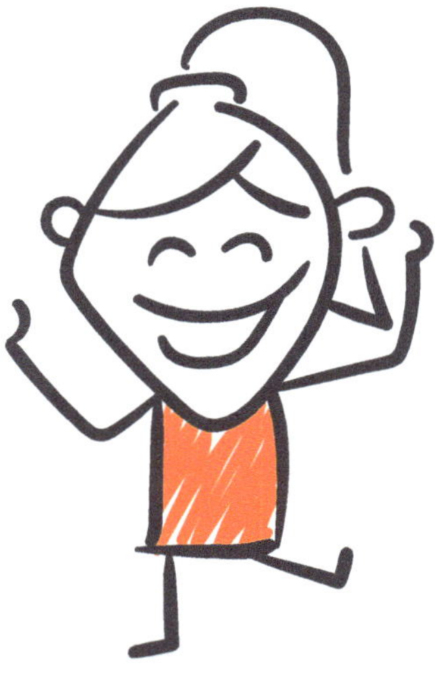

RED Tape : Rules and forms that get in the way of getting things done.

RED Blood Cells : The RED part of our blood that stores oxygen.

RED Hot : So hot it GLOWS.

RED Alert : It means that something bad could happen.

RED Cross : A group that helps people in disasters.

RED Ribbon : An award for coming in second in a competition.

Seeing **RED** : Being bothered, irritated or annoyed.

RED Sox : A professional baseball team from Boston.

RED Brass : Brass with enough copper to give it a reddish tint.

RED Neck : An uneducated person living in the countryside.

RED Letter : Something that deserves extra attention - Red Letter Days.

RED Flag : Used as a warning of danger.

RED Line : Is the recommended safety limit.

RED Carpet : Used for important guests.

RED Planet : Nickname for Mars, the 4th planet in our solar system.

RED Giant : A very large star with low surface temperature.

Paint the town **RED** : To go out and celebrate wildly.

RED Tide : When the ocean turns reddish because of an algae

RED Ink : Used in reference to being in debt.

Code **RED** : A warning signal indicating danger.

RED Card : In soccer and other games a red card indicates a player is ejected.

RED Shift : When light waves shift towards red because they are moving away from earth.

Little **RED** Riding Hood : A fairy tale of a girl who meets a wolf.

in the **RED** : Owing more money than what is earned. Being in debt.

RED Dwarf : A small, old and relatively cool star.

RED Letter Day : A day that is pleasantly noteworthy or memorable.

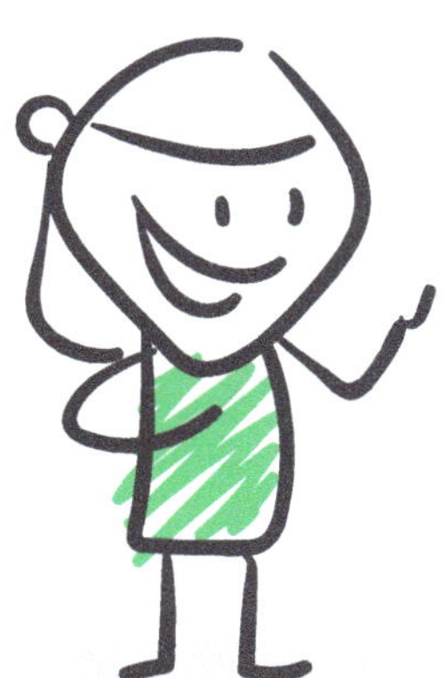

Now we have **GREEN**.
Read on and see,
GREEN is important.
You'll have to agree.

GREEN Room : A room in a theater where performers can relax when they are not performing.

GREEN Space : An area of grass, trees, and other vegetation set apart for recreation.

GREEN Party : An environmental political party.

Go **GREEN** : Making more environmentally friendly choices.

GREEN Goddess : A salad dressing made with parsley and green onions.

GREEN Manure : A fertilizer consisting of growing plants that are plowed back into the soil.

GREEN Box : A large metal container for disposal and recycling of electronic waste.

GREEN Thumb : A natural talent for growing plants.

GREEN Revolution : A large increase in crop production in developing countries achieved by the use of fertilizers, pesticides, and high-yield crop varieties.

GREEN Soap : A soft soap made from vegetable oils and used especially in the treatment of skin diseases.

GREEN Card : A permit allowing a foreign national to live and work permanently in the US.

GREEN Belt : An area of open land around a city.

GREEN Beret : A member of the U.S. army special forces.

GREEN Market : Selling products or services based on their environmental benefit.

GREEN Acres : An American comedy TV show from 1965 - 1971.

GREEN Bay Packers : An American professional football team from Wisconsin.

GREENhorn : A person who is new or inexperienced at a particular activity.

GREENhouse : A glass building in which plants are grown.

GREENback : A U.S. dollar bill.

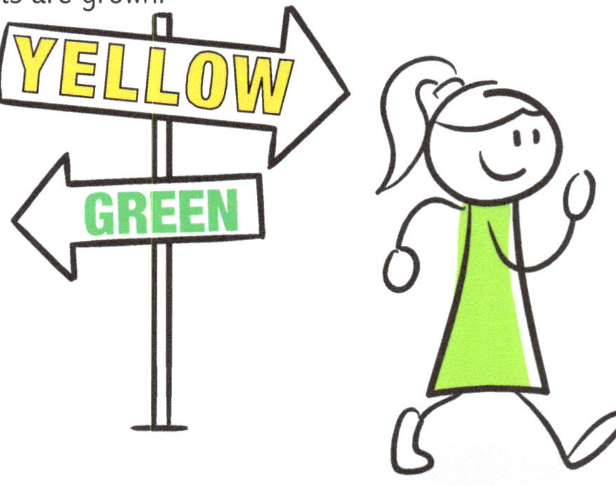

Let's look at YELLOW.
Let's look at the ways
it's used in our writing
and the things that we say.

YELLOW Brick Road : A golden road found in the story, "The Wizard of Oz".

YELLOW Fever : A disease carried by mosquitoes causing fever and a yellowing of the skin.

YELLOW Flag : A flag indicating quarantine on a ship and a danger warning for drivers.

YELLOW Belly : A way to call someone a coward.

YELLOW Streak : A tendency to be afraid or easily scared.

YELLOW Pages : The business pages of phone book or, now, an online business directory.

YELLOW Journalism : News reporting based on crude exaggeration.

YELLOW Jacket : A wasp or hornet with yellow markings.

YELLOW Dog : A cowardly person or thing.

YELLOWhammer : In baseball ; a curve ball. Also a type of bird.

Look at the phrases.
Oh, what would we do,
if we took out the word -
the color word BLUE?

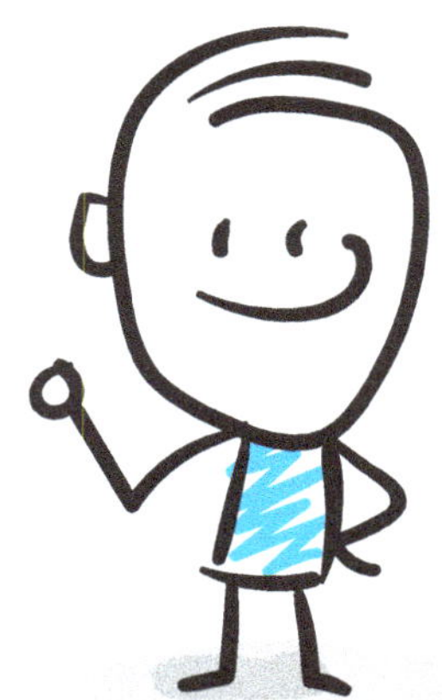

BLUE Jay: A type of bird.

BLUE Chip : Considered good. Usually in reference to a company on the stock market.

BLUE Blood : A person of noble birth.

BLUE Funk : A state of depression.

BLUE Collar : Relating to manual work or workers.

BLUE Smoke : Means an engine is burning too much oil.

BLUE Streak : Something that moves very fast.

True **BLUE** : Extremely loyal.

BLUE Jets : A discharge of blue light from the top of a thunderstorm.

BLUE Flag : A European award for clean and safe beaches. Also, a flower.

BLUE Cheese : A type of cheese.

Once in a **BLUE** Moon : Very rarely.

BLUE Line : One of two lines on an ice hockey rink.

BLUE Ice : Clean blue ice formed by glaciers.

BLUE Bonnet : A Scottish hat, a flower and a brand of margarine.

BLUE Pencil : To edit or make changes to a writing or movie.

Big **BLUE** : A nickname for the IBM company.

BLUE Moon : A 2nd full in moon in a month or when the moon looks blue due to smoke or dust.

BLUE Peter : A flag raised by a ship that is about to leave port.

BLUE Book : A book listing the prices of used cars or a blank book used for tests.

BLUE Ribbon : A prize given to first place. Also means of high quality or first class.

BLUE Giant : A large bluish star with a surface temperature hotter than our sun.

BLUE Flu : When police officers strike or call in sick.

BLUE Angels : The United States Navy's flight demonstration squadron.

BLUE Ridge Mountains : A range in the Appalachian mountains.

BLUE Jeans : Pants made from blue denim.

BLUEgrass : A kind of country music.

BLUEprint : A design or other technical drawing.

The **BLUE**S : A type or style of music of black American folk origin.

BLUE Chip Stocks : Stock of a large brand name company.

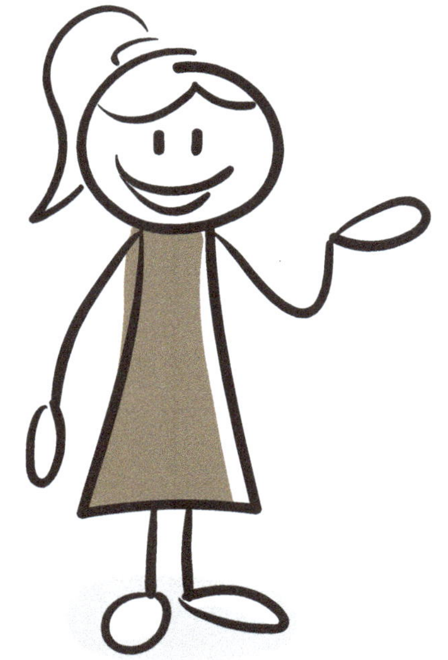

BROWN is used, too.
But, not like the rest.
Compared to the others,
it's clearly not best.

BROWN Nose : To act overly favorably in order to get something.

BROWNout: A reduction or restriction of electrical power.

BROWN Bag(ging) : To take a packed lunch to work or school.

BROWN Bread : Bread made from unbleached whole wheat.

BROWN Sugar : Unrefined sugar.

BROWN Dwarf : Found in space and is the size of a large planet or a small star.

BROWN Earth : A type of soil rich in humus.

BROWN Creeper : A plant that creeps along the ground, around another plant or up a wall.

BROWN Betty : A baked pudding made from fruit and breadcrumbs.

BROWN Goods: Television sets, audio equipment, and similar household appliances

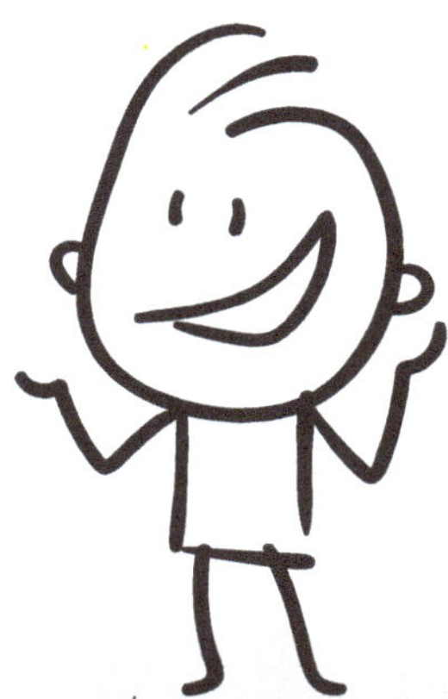

BLACK and WHITE.
Both are used, too.
To describe some things
we say and do.

BLACKout : Losing electrical power or losing consciousness.

BLACK Diamond : A lump of coal.

BLACK Eye : Bruised skin around the eye.

BLACK Forest : A famous wooded area in southwest Germany.

BLACK Market : Buying and selling illegally.

BLACK Maria : A police vehicle for transporting prisoners.

BLACK Ops : A secret operation by the military that might do things that are usually illegal.

BLACK Tie : A black bow tie usually worn with a tuxedo.

BLACK Bread : A dark colored type of rye bread.

BLACK Flag : Either a pirates flag or a motor sports flag to signal drivers to stop immediately.

BLACK Jack : A card game where players try to add cards up to 21.

BLACK Humor : A type of comedy that makes fun of unfortunate situations etc.

BLACK Sea : A large sea located between east Asia and West Asia.

BLACK Letter : A typeset or font also known as Gothic.

BLACK Bag : A bag that doctors use to use to carry instruments and drugs.

BLACK Hole : A collapsed star that has gravity so strong that even light can not escape it.

BLACK Friday : The day after Thanksgiving that has stores giving special deals.

BLACK-Eyed Susan : Any number of flowers that have yellow petals and dark centers.

BLACK Light : A type of light bulb that emits ultra-violet light which is invisible to the eye.

BLACK Belt : A belt worn by an expert in Judo, Karate or other martial arts.

BLACKmail : Is an act of trying to make someone do something because of a threat.

BLACK Box : A flight recorder in an airplane.

BLACK Sheep : A member of a family or group that is viewed as a disgrace.

BLACK Magic : Magic that supposedly involves witchcraft or evil spirits.

BLACK Book : A private book that contains a list of secret names or contacts.

BLACK Death : A great epidemic of bubonic plague that hit in the mid 14th century.

BLACK Ice : A layer of nearly invisible ice - usually found on roads.

BLACK Monday : The stock market crash of Monday, October 19, 1987.

BLACK Gold : Another name for oil or petroleum.

WHITE Gold : A silver colored alloy of gold.

WHITE Noise : Hissing, buzzing or soothing background noise.

WHITE Pages : The part of a phone book that has residential phone numbers.

WHITE Water : Fast shallow stretches of water (rapids) in a river.

WHITE Matter : Brain and spinal cord tissue.

WHITE Space : The un-printed area of a piece of printing.

WHITE Christmas : A Christmas with snow on the ground.

WHITE Elephant Gift : A gift that someone has not bought new.

WHITE House : The house where the United States president lives.

WHITE Goods: Large electrical goods like refrigerators and washing machines.

WHITE Collar : Refers to the workers, or things done, in an office setting.

WHITE Out : A heavy snowstorm or becoming impaired by exposure to sudden bright light.

WHITE Lie : A trivial or harmless lie.

WHITE Knight : A person that helps someone.

WHITE hot : Something so hot that it glows white.

WHITE Horse : A wave that is broken by the wind.

WHITE Flag : A cloth or flag waved as a symbol of surrender.

Snow WHITE : Of pure white color or the kindhearted princess in a Disney movie.

WHITE Knuckle : Something that causes excitement or fear.

WHITE Glove : Involving tremendous care, attention, service or cleanliness.

WHITE Sale : When a store puts household linens on sale.

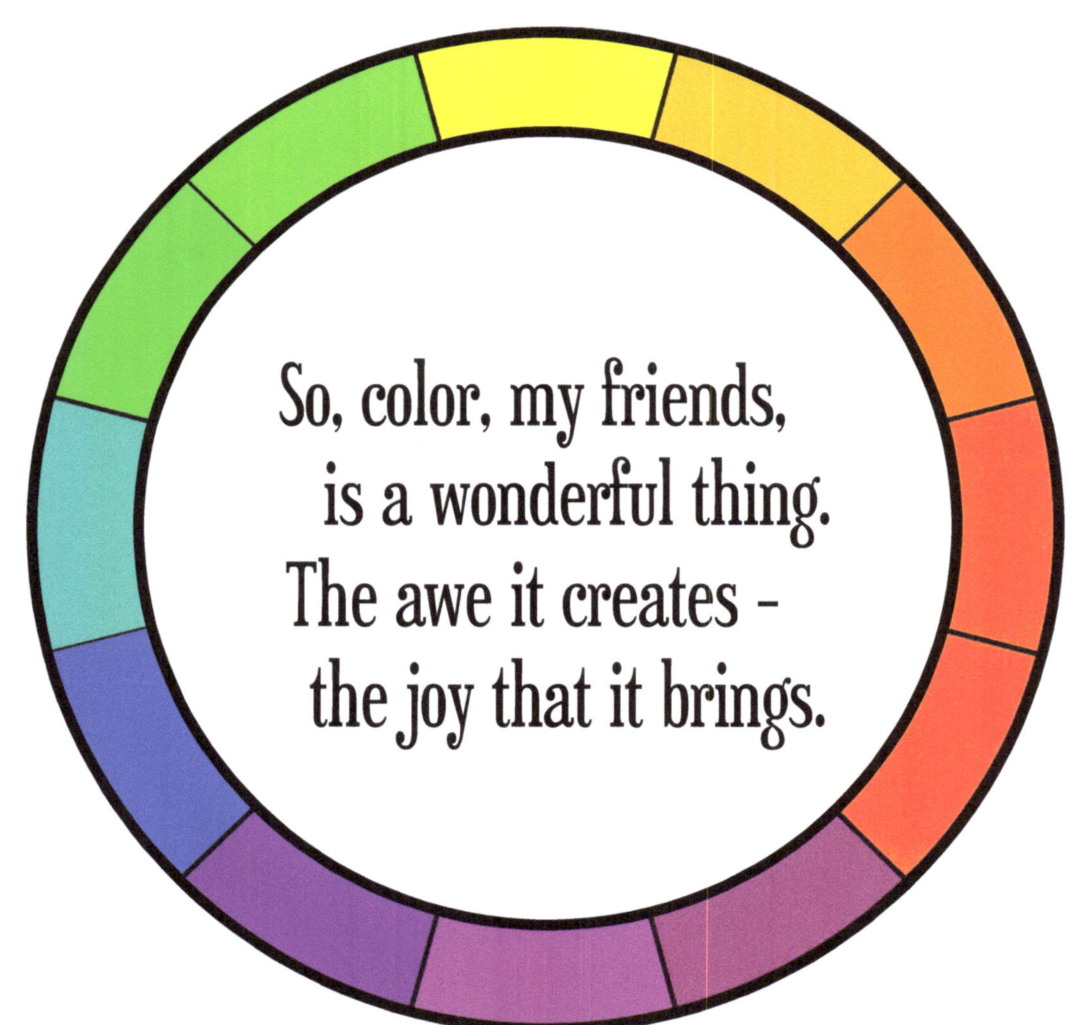

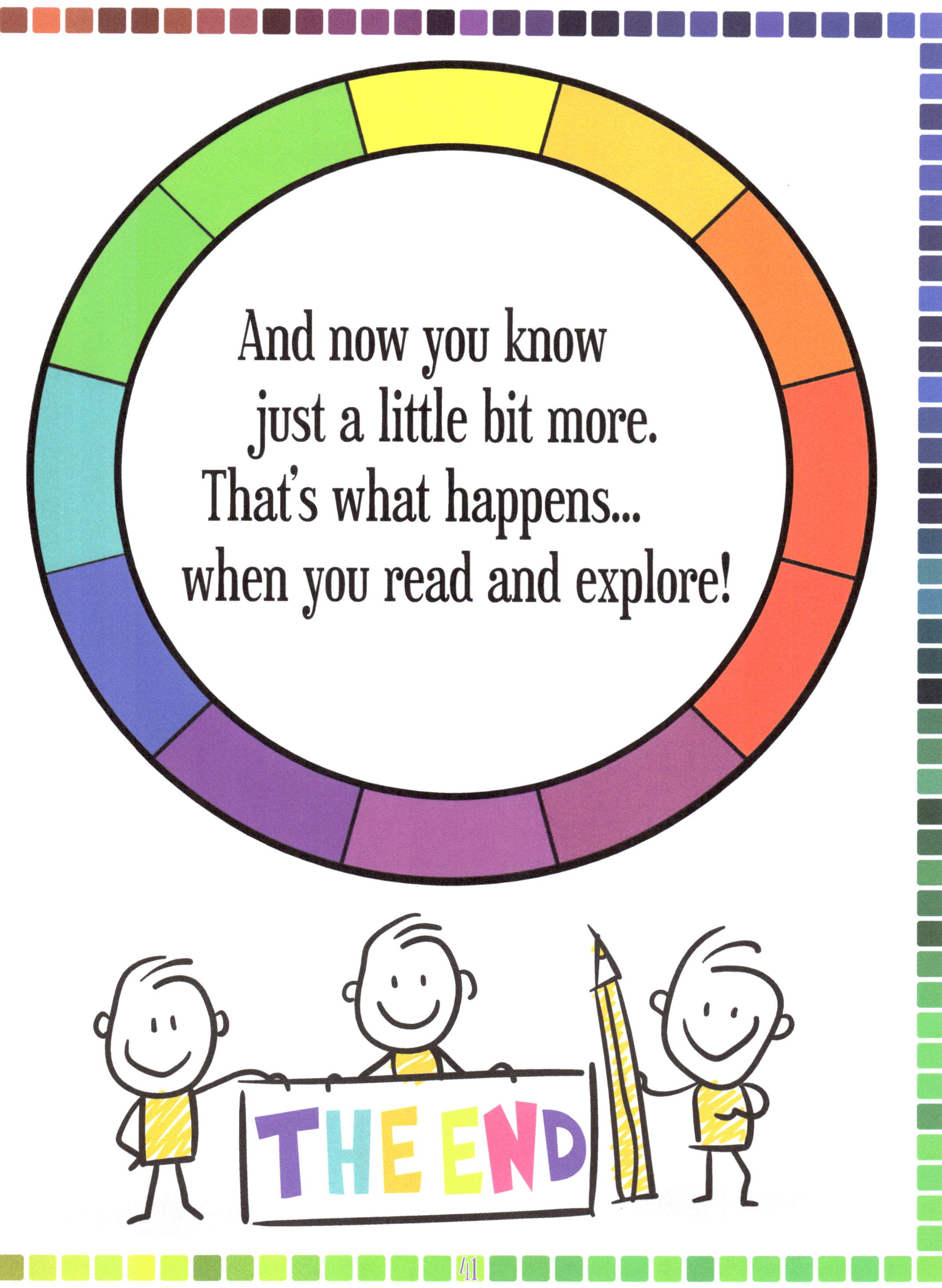

And now you know
just a little bit more.
That's what happens...
when you read and explore!

THE END

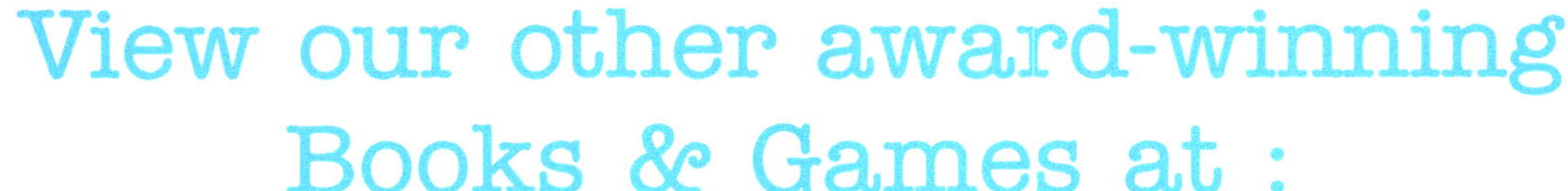

View our other award-winning
Books & Games at :

MissingPiecePress.com

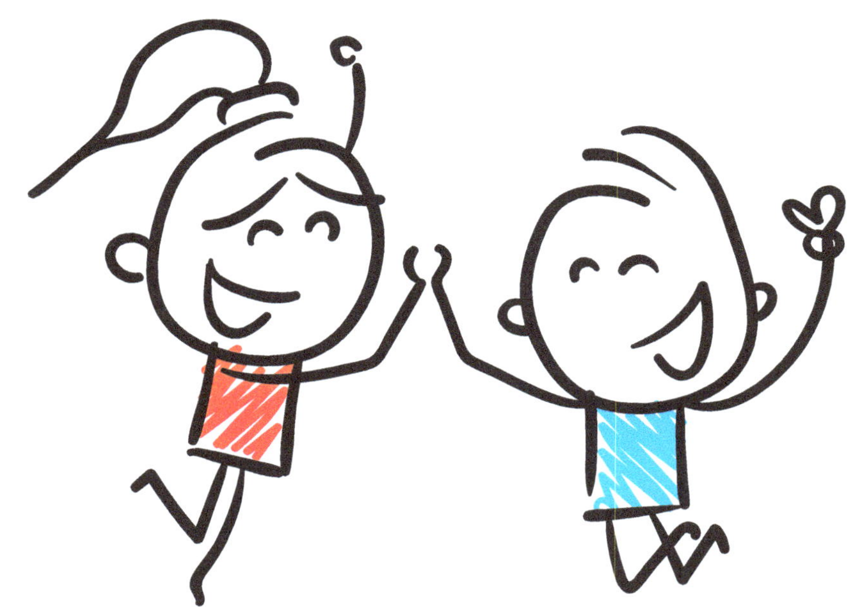